THE GUTSY EXECUTIVE COACH
FUNCTIONAL NUTRITION • CBT HYPNOTHERAPY

gutsyexecutivecoach.com

Welcome

This workbook is designed to accompany the Heal Your Gut online program. My intention for you is that within the next few weeks, **you begin to see what is possible** for your life, when you're no longer pre-occupied with worrying about what to eat, how you feel or how you look.

Together, we'll explore the foundations of creating health, so that you can live with **more energy**, less stress, and **more joy.**

You'll change your story by changing your **thoughts**, **words**, and your **vision** for your future, so that life abundantly becomes your reality.

GET THE BODY RIGHT, AND THE BRAIN WILL FOLLOW
GET THE BRAIN RIGHT, AND THE MIND WILL FOLLOW
- Dr. Daniel Amen

My Vision

With the information you'll be learning, **you're going to see that you don't need to be defined by a diagnosis or symptoms.**

So **let's start** by seeing yourself as you **would like to look, feel, and be...** and feel free to revisit this vision weekly, monthly and quarterly!

WHAT IS **MY VISION** FOR THE NEXT MONTH?

HOW DO I WANT TO FEEL IN MY BODY & MY MIND?

GENERAL **PRINCIPLES OF HEALTH BUILDING**
OUTPERFORMS SPECIFIC TREATMENTS
- Reed Davis, Founder FDN

My Intentions

People who **set intentions are 10x more likely to see them become reality.** There are 365 Days in a year, and **every passing minute is a chance to turn things around.**

Small, **M**easurable, **A**ctionable, **R**esults-Oriented and **T**ime Specific **(SMART)** Goals can help you really take right action!

WHAT **ONE THING** WILL I FOCUS ON IN THE NEXT WEEK?

WHO WILL KEEP ME ACCOUNTABLE?

HOW WILL **I CELEBRATE** ONCE I'VE ACHIEVED IT?

I AM FEARFULLY AND **WONDERFULLY MADE**
- Psalm 139:14

Break through Barriers

WHAT ARE **MY BARRIERS** TO SUCCESS?

HOW MUCH TIME DO I SPEND DOING THINGS THAT STEAL MY TIME?

WHAT ARE **MY DISTRACTIONS**?

Setting Gutsy Goals

WHAT DO **I REALLY WANT?**

WHY DO I WANT IT?

HOW WILL I FEEL ONCE I ACHIEVE IT

"**EVERYTHING IS ENERGY** AND THAT'S ALL THERE IS TO IT. MATCH THE FREQUENCY OF THE REALITY YOU WANT AND **YOU CANNOT HELP BUT GET THAT REALITY**. IT CAN BE NO OTHER WAY. THIS IS NOT PHILOSOPHY. THIS IS PHYSICS."
- Albert Einstein, Genius

Embedding the Vision

Now that you've crafted this on paper, it's time to put it into practice.

Did you know that your mind doesn't know the difference between what's real and what's imagined?

So with this guided visualization, you're going to start training your mind to align with the reality of what you want, activating your brain's **Reticular Activation System (RAS).**

SCAN THIS CODE TO DOWNLOAD

The Blueprint

You'll be amazed what can change within 90 days. But there are phases, and these are collectively referred to as the 7R Protocol. The first phase will be **supporting the body's mitochondria. This diagram is your roadmap** so you know what each phase represents, and what to expect.

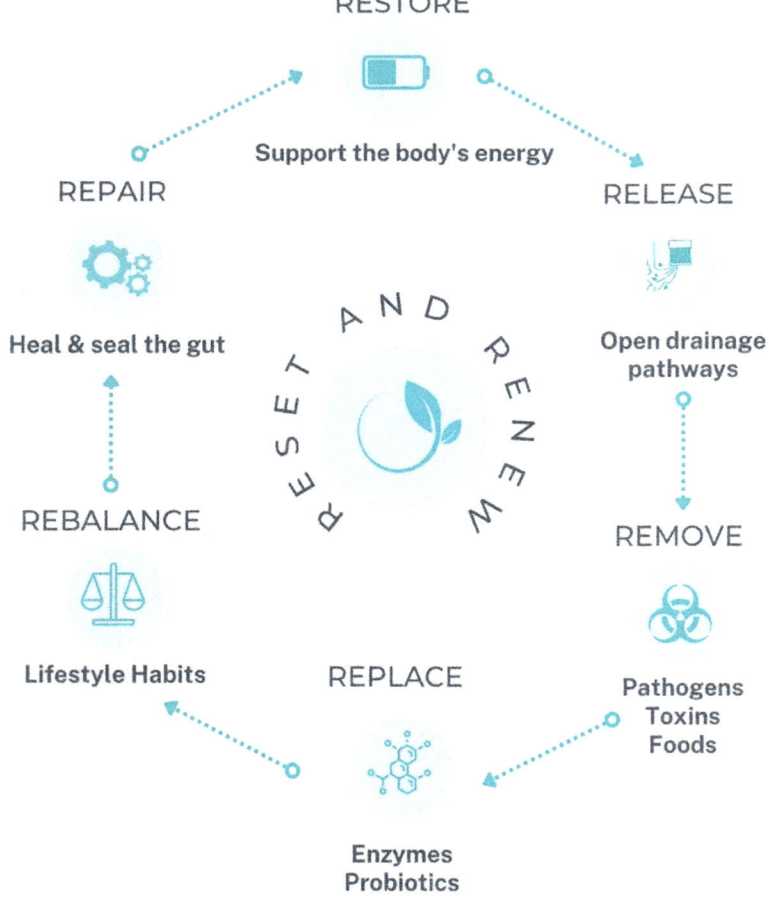

RESTORE

Support the body's energy

REPAIR

Heal & seal the gut

RELEASE

Open drainage pathways

RESET AND RENEW

REMOVE

Pathogens
Toxins
Foods

REBALANCE

Lifestyle Habits

REPLACE

Enzymes
Probiotics

NEARLY ALL OF THE CHRONIC DISEASES THAT CAUSE SO MUCH SUFFERING AND ARE STEADILY DRIVING UP THE COST OF HEALTH CARE, **ALL SHARE MITOCHONDRIAL DYSFUNCTION**, EXCESSIVE INFLAMMATION, HIGH CORTISOL LEVELS, AND OTHER MARKERS OF BROKEN BIOCHEMISTRY.
- Dr Terry Wahls, Author The Wahls Protocol

D

I

E

T

My Metabolic Type

When you eat more in line with your genetic requirements, you're able to create energy. This is what we call eating for your Metabolic Type.

Energy is the first marker of health. If you notice you eat something then end up needing a nap within 2 hours, that's a clue you haven't been eating right your type, your blood sugar is off, or you're sensitive to that food.

If you've been eating low fat, low protein and high carb, but you're a Fast Oxidizer, you'll feel pretty burnt out and will likely snack a lot because you're not getting what you need from your food.

You'll be customizing your nutrition firstly by **eating for your Metabolic Type**, and using the Diet Check Record below to notice how you feel after each meal or snack so you can determine if that meal was satisfying your metabolic requirements.

Diet Check Record

Use this 1 - 2 hours after **each** meal to see if your new eating habits are stabilizing your blood sugar and you're getting the energy you need from your food.

- [ ] Feel full and satisfied
- [ ] Do NOT have sweet cravings
- [ ] Do NOT desire more food
- [ ] Do NOT feel hungry
- [ ] Do NOT need to snack before next meal
- [ ] Energy feels renewed
- [ ] Have good, lasting, "normal" sense of energy
- [ ] Improved well-being
- [ ] Sense of feeling refueled, renewed and restored
- [ ] Some emotional upliftment
- [ ] Improved mental clarity and sharpness
- [ ] Normalization of thought processes
- [ ] Feel physically full (bloated), but still hungry
- [ ] Craving something sweet
- [ ] Not satisfied, feel like something was missing
- [ ] Already hungry
- [ ] Feel the need for a snack
- [ ] Meal gave too much or too little energy
- [ ] Became hyper, jittery, shaky, nervous or speedy
- [ ] Felt hyper, but exhausted "underneath"
- [ ] Energy dip - exhaustion, sleepiness, drowsiness, listlessness or lethargy
- [ ] Mentally slow, sluggish, or spacy
- [ ] Inability to think quickly or clearly
- [ ] Hyper, overly rapid thoughts
- [ ] Inability to focus or concentrate
- [ ] Apathy, depression, withdrawal or sadness
- [ ] Anxious, obsessive, fearful, angry or irritable

Visit MTDIET.COM to learn more

My Sensitivities

Secondly, you'll be removing the foods that you're sensitive to. Eating foods that you are intolerant to can really zap you of energy.

A sensitivity to most foods can be felt **within a couple hours** but **as much as 72 hours after eating**. For **gluten,** it can be even longer... **up to 96 days!**

And this will really blow your mind!

Not all food sensitivities show up in digestion. They can show up as neuro-psychological issues, poor vision, and skin conditions like eczema, hives and psoriasis.

Why? Because the liver becomes congested from dealing with multiple stressors.

I'm suggesting you remove known inflammatory foods like **Dairy, Gluten, Sugar and Alcohol,** for a minimum of 14 days because they drain the body of its energy. It's common to begin feeling noticeably better within the first 7 - 14 days, once you're putting back in nutrients and minerals.

Hydrate

We often forget how important it is for us to stay hydrated. As little as a **2% drop in hydration** impairs performance in tasks that require attention, psychomotor and memory skills, as well as the ability to make decisions. **Adding a small pinch of Redmond's or Celtic grey sea salt** to your water will amplify your hydration efforts and support your adrenals.

KEEP **A 500ml BOTTLE OF WATER** NEXT TO YOUR BED AND **TAKE A FEW SIPS ON WAKING**

EAT **CELERY, CUCUMBERS, AND WATERMELON** OR OTHER WATER RICH FOODS TO SUPPLEMENT YOUR FLUID INTAKE

WATER IS LIFE'S MATTER AND MATRIX, MOTHER AND MEDIUM. **THERE IS NO LIFE WITHOUT WATER**.
- Albert Szent Gyorgi

Purified Water

Mastering the basics includes Purified Water. I'm a personal fan of Distilled water, as tap water contains several undesirable chemicals and potential pathogens that are contraindicated to creating health.

For my favorite Water Distiller, **SCAN THE CODE**

Protein

The building block of your **neurotransmitters and your hormones.** Consuming more protein with each meal will not only **make you more emotionally balanced,** but also satiated. Chemically, you are **slowing down** the conversion of **glucose** and balancing your blood sugar. You're also supporting Phase 2 Liver Detoxification!

CHICKEN BREAST
10g Protein

FISH
22g Protein

WHOLE EGG
13g Protein

RED MEAT
18g Protein

REAL FOOD DOESN'T HAVE INGREDIENTS
REAL FOOD IS INGREDIENTS
- Jamie Oliver

Essential Fats

Your brain is made up of **60% fat**. Your hormones are made from **B Vitamins and Cholesterol!** Therefore, good fats are vital for health. They carry, absorb, and store **fat-soluble vitamins (A, D, E, and K)** in your bloodstream.

If ever you've been low in Vitamin A or D, consider drizzling your vegetables in Extra Virgin Olive or Coconut Oil. If you can tolerate it, organic, grass-fed butter is also a healthful option!

Almond Butter	Avocado	Chia Seeds
Coconut	Free Range Eggs	Flax Seeds
Nuts (Walnuts)	Olives	Salmon

Energy Lifters

Thiamine **(Vitamin B1)** - Decreased levels affect mitochondrial activity (aka the powerhouse of the cell) thereby decreasing energy production. Find it in black beans and cauliflower.

Vitamin B6 - Low levels correlate with the brain using less glucose to produce energy and disrupts brain cell communication. Incorporate more eggs, chicken, and watermelon to add in B6!

Folate **(Vitamin B9)** - A deficiency disrupts cell development meaning your body requires more energy for normal activity. Find it in dark leafy greens like spinach and asparagus.

Vitamin B12 - You can't get this on a plant-based diet so choose beef, eggs, and salmon. It will keep your nervous system in check. **If you choose to supplement - it's wise to get your genetics checked** so you know which form of B12 to use.

Vitamin C - This essential antioxidant is vital for energy, and for helping the liver. If levels are low, it can lead to fatigue and low immunity.Find it in camu camu, broccoli, brussels sprouts, and kiwis!

Vitamin D - When deficient, inflammation occurs and your brain can be damaged. You'll mostly get it from sunlight but food sources include mushrooms, sardines, and egg yolks. If you're supplementing, you require Vitamin K2 and Magnesium to help it convert.

Vitamin E - If you have a digestive disorder you may become deficient in this vitamin, causing problems for nervous system development. Find it in almonds, spinach, and sunflower seeds!

Zinc - Zinc deficiency is fairly common and is a hallmark of chronic fatigue syndrome. Seafood, namely oysters.

Magnesium - Decreases inflammation and relaxes the nervous system. Find it in Almonds, Avocados, Buckwheat and Cacao.

Liver Support

DHEA, Estrogen, Progesterone and Testosterone make up your sex hormones. If you experience issues like headaches, acne, sore boobs, or night sweats, it can indicate an imbalance in your sex hormones and a **sign of liver congestion**. Helping the liver out with supportive foods will reduce the stress the body is under.

NAC – which is sulfur rich – is found in eggs, while glutathione can be found in Rooibos Tea. You may also need to supplement NAC and Glutathione to **reach the required levels if you're not absorbing adequately through food.**

Reduce Alcohol   Brassicas   Citrus

Antioxidants   Reduce junk food   Dandelion Tea

Filtered Water   Oily Fish   NAC + Selenium

Healthy Hormones

Painful periods, heavy periods, endometriosis, PCOS, and PMS can indicate estrogen dominance. Periods that just go and on can indicate a lack of progesterone. Consuming **Bitter Greens** and **Pink or Purple** Vegetables combined with **B Vitamins & animal protein, maca root powder, pumpkin seeds, flaxseeds, sunflower seeds and sesame seeds, regulating blood sugar and cortisol** will support healthier sex hormones. But you may need to consider certain supplements or bio-identical hormone replacement (bHRT).

Bok Choy

Brussel Sprouts

Cabbage

Carrots

Cauliflower

Collard Greens

Mustard Greens

Radish

Turnips

GREEN ISN'T JUST A LUCKY COLOUR. **IT'S A KEY NUTRIENT FOR YOUR BRAIN AND MENTAL HEALTH**
- Dr Uma Naidoo

Nitric Oxide

We measure oxidative stress with the Metabolic Wellness Panel, which will tells you how your cells are aging and if there is damage to your DNA.

Vegetables like arugula, beetroot and celery are packed with nitrates, which are **converted to nitric oxide (NO)** in your body. NO promotes vasodilation, improving cardio vascular health, making the blood vessels a little more full and **lowering blood pressure**. It is crucial to maintain the required levels of NO as it supports stem cell activation and can slow down or reverse telomere shortening, therefore preventing brain degeneration.

A **telomere** is the end of a chromosome. **Telomeres** are made of repetitive sequences of non-coding DNA that protect the chromosome from damage. Nitric oxide has an anti-aging effect on telomeres.

One of the easiest ways to improve NO Production is while we sleep by **inhaling and exhaling through the nose**. But there are lots of ways to to improve NO, including supplementation.

| Arugula | Beetroot | Celery |
| HIIT | Mouth Taping | Redlight |

Reducing Toxins

We're surrounded by **chemicals and toxins** in our air, water, **personal care products**, pots and pans, **electromagnetic radiation** from our smart phones, computers and microwaves, and our food.

While you're not always in control of the air, you can take steps to **reduce toxic exposure by starting with food.** These are the foods that are sprayed with the most pesticides, so ***always*** buy the organic versions of these.

Apples

Celery

Cherries

Collard Greens, Kale, Mustard Greens

Grapes

Nectarines

Peaches

Pears

Peppers

Spinach

Strawberries

Tomatoes

Healthy Swaps

This bread mix has only 5 ingredients. Made with coconut and almond flour, all you add is a little olive or coconut oil and eggs / flax eggs.

Regular Bread

Gluten-Free Bread

This penne contains only red lentil so it's a safer option than some of the other corn-based or rice-based products.

Regular Pasta

Gluten-Free Pasta

WHATEVER YOU ARE NOT **CHANGING**, YOU ARE **CHOOSING**
- Dr Nasha Winters

Grocery Hacks

Remember to pick up vegetables that will last. Consider fresh produce that has a longer shelf-life like **Cabbage, Carrots, Onions, Oranges, Peppers, Sweet Potatoes and Tomatoes.**

Find organic **frozen broccoli, cauliflower, asparagus, sugar snap peas** and even freeze some yourself, so they keep longer, and all you need to do is steam or lightly cook them for 5 minutes when you're ready.

Order **Organic Grass Fed Beef** from **Piedmontese,** Beef Sticks from **Paleo Valley,** and Wild Caught Fish from **Wild Alaskan**.

MASTERY IS NOT A DESTINATION. **IT'S AN EVOLUTION**
- Christine Kane

Beautiful Skin

Since older cells are constantly shed and replaced by younger ones, your body needs a steady supply of key nutrients to support this rapid growth. Feed your skin the vital nutrients it needs to help it stay soft, supple, wrinkle-free and blemish-free.

Vitamin A in Liver

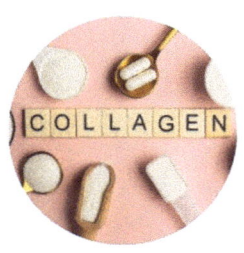

Collagen

Vitamin C

Vitamin E

Exercise

Omega 3s

Sleep

Reduce Stress

Sunlight

Invitation

Check out The Gutsy Community where you can share your goals with like-minded Gutsy women.

This is a safe place to journey through this experience together.

SCAN THIS CODE TO JOIN

R

E

S

T

Rest

Have you heard the expression, **REST for SUCCESS?** So often with our frantic 21st Century lives, we're always on, always being notified by our devices, and very rarely feel like we can enjoy downtime **without feeling guilty.**

This state of **constantly doing - and overdoing** - can leave us feeling **frazzled,** and is disruptive of our Hormones, Immunity, Memory, Metabolism and Mood (**H.I.M.M.**)

IN ORDER FOR THE BODY TO HEAL,
IT HAS TO BE IN A HEALING STATE
- Alex Howard

Quality & Quantity

Quality - as well as quantity – of rest is important. The average adult is sleeping less than 7 hours per night. We're sleeping **less than our grandparents** due to the stresses of modern life.

The list below highlights some of the most important things you can do to improve both your quality and quantity of sleep.

- Morning Sunlight
- No lights or screens 2 hours before bed
- Eat a blood-sugar balancing dinner
- Supplements like magnesium or melatonin
- A Cool, Calm, Clean Bedroom

HOW MANY OF THESE **THINGS ARE YOU DOING?**

IS THERE ANYTHING YOU CAN **BEGIN DOING NOW?**

Sleep Tracker

One of the most helpful things I've ever done is to invest in the Oura Ring. Sleep Stages, Activity, HRV recovery, Body temperature, Heart Rate, Respiratory Rate, Cycle tracking — it factors in all of the major facets of women's health!

You'll learn pretty quickly where your sleep strengths lie, and what you need to work on. Oura considers your sleep timing to be optimal and aligned with the sun when the midpoint of your sleep falls between midnight and 3am, so it teaches you to work with your circadian rhythm.

SCAN TO SAVE $50 OFF YOUR OURA RING

GREAT DAYS BEGIN WITH **A GREAT NIGHT'S SLEEP**
- Anonymous

Sleep Deeper MP3

Download the Sleep Deeper Mp3 onto your desktop computer and save to your preferred Music phone app.

SCAN ME

This way when you sync with your phone, so you can access the file on both the phone and the computer!

Set aside 10 minutes once you get into bed.

Put your headphones in.

Breathe slowly and deeply.

Listen to the sound of my voice.

Drift off to sleep.

If you do wake in the middle of the night, repeat.

Suggested Rituals

Making **sleep a priority** is one of the first steps to improving your quality and quantity of sleep. Having a routine is impactful. These are the ones that work for me, that I've curated from numerous sources.

7am	Drink mineral rich, distilled water
7:15am	15 mins sunlight to boost natural melatonin production
7:30am	Move your body for 30 minutes
8am	10 minutes slow breathing
12pm	No more caffeine, choose Tulsi tea instead
4pm	60 Minutes Restorative Exercise
5pm	No more alcohol
6:30pm	Dinner balanced for your Metabolic Type
7pm	Watch the sunset
7:30pm	Dim white overhead lights
8pm	Disconnect from devices
8:30pm	Magnesium foot bath
9pm	Gratitude journal
9:30pm	Slow breathing
10pm	Sleep in a cool, dark room for deep sleep

EXERCISE

Over-Exercise

While I generally **encourage daily movement,** it's also important to check in with your body that this is **not creating additional stress**. Examine how you feel **1 - 2 hours after exercise**. If you feel **drained and exhausted, you've done too much.**

The **best time of day for intense exercise** is either first thing in the **morning** or **mid afternoon**.

Anything **from 5pm onward** should be geared towards more restorative practices like **Restorative Pilates.**

Avoid hot yoga, long runs or cardio in the evenings, as this elevates your heart rate, disrupts blood sugar and will **inhibit restful sleep.**

Remember the 3Ps

Exercise is a wonderful addition to any health-promoting routine. It's part of the **3Ps of Detoxification** - Peeing, Pooping & **Perspiring**.

If you exercise **but fail to perspire**, you need to investigate why, and then focus on optimizing this detox pathway. **Lymph drainage** is vital to your healing!

ARE YOU CURRENTLY **SWEATING 5 TIMES PER WEEK?**

HOW CAN YOU **ADD MORE SWEATY** WORKOUTS?

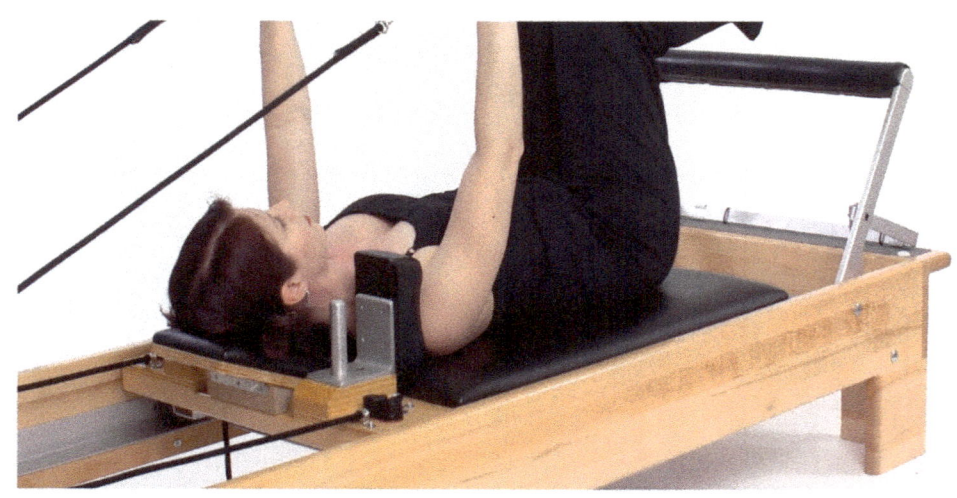

Interval Training

If your **adrenals are healthy**, then engage in **Sprint Interval Training (SIT)** or **High Intensity Interval Training (HIIT)**

SELECT ONE OR MORE OF THESE THAT YOU ENJOY:

- RUNNING, SPINNING, REBOUNDING, ROWING

- GO ALL OUT FOR 1 MINUTE THEN **REST FOR 3 MIN.**

- **REPEAT 4 - 8 TIMES** TO WORK UP A SWEAT

- TOTAL TIME: **15 - 30 MINUTES**

START AT **ONCE PER WEEK** THEN BUILD TO **5 TIMES**

Strength Training

As you get older, you lose muscle mass, which is crucial for maintaining a healthy body weight and sex hormones like testosterone. Strength training should **begin with body weight** and or band exercise, **until you're able to work with weights.** Start small **then build to 3 times** per week.

 BEGIN WITH A **10 MINUTE WARM UP**

THEN MOVE ON TO **PLANKS, PUSH UPS, PULL DOWNS**

WORK WITH A PERSONAL TRAINER FOR CORRECT FORM

5 – 8 REPS FOR **3 SETS**

ADD (**SUPERVISED**) LOAD EVERY 2 – 3 WEEKS

Restorative Exercise

Stretching throughout the day and incorporating **slow breathing can help with opening tight muscles**, while getting oxygen into the your cells, which can **reduce stress.**

You can also **engage in fluid, dynamic exercises** to not only nurture your body, but **also your spirit.**

SELECT **ONE OR MORE** OF THESE THAT **YOU ENJOY:**

DANCE, RESTORATIVE PILATES, TAI CHI

If **burnout is a problem for you,** then doing **more of this type of exercise** will be **better for you,** than the Interval Training mentioned.

Remember: examine how you feel 1 - 2 hours after exercise. If you feel drained and exhausted, you've done too much or it's not the right form of activity for you.

S
T
R
E
S
S

Stress Reduction

Did you know that there are **3 types of stressors that you need to be aware of?**

- **Physical** - Accidents, falls, injuries and trauma

- **Biochemical** - Viruses, bacteria, hormones in foods, heavy metals, mold, hangovers and blood sugar imbalances

- **Psycho-emotional** - relationships, family, career, and finances

All organisms in nature **can tolerate short-term stress**, but **humans are the only ones who can regulate stress by thought alone.**

WHICH OF THESE 3 APPLIES TO YOU?

Stress & Burn-Out

Whichever of the 3 kinds of stress you're dealing with, if left unaddressed, it inevitably leads to a state of **adreno-cortical exhaustion** or **"burn-out."**

There's **no one quick fix, no single herb or nutrient** – which unfortunately, we've been conditioned to expect, as a result of the standard western approach, which will **address only one aspect of the problem, rather than all the contributors.**

Doctors simply **match a symptom to a drug,** and in the case of some nutritional therapists, **they'll match a symptom to a vitamin or a herb.** This provides symptom relief, but fails to address the underlying WHY.

Functional diagnostics can help identify the biochemical causes, but what about the psychological.

ARE THERE UNDERLYING THOUGHT PATTERNS DRIVING YOUR STRESS?

CAN YOU IDENTIFY WHEN THIS BEGAN?

WAS THERE A TRIGGERING EVENT?

Identifying Stressors

WHAT DO YOU IDENTIFY AS PERCEIVED THREATS?

WHAT SYMPTOMS DO YOU EXPERIENCE?

WHEN WAS THE LAST TIME YOU FELT CALM?

Slow Breathing

One of the best ways of addressing psychological stress is to bring your autonomic nervous system back into balance **via the breath.**

Noticing the quality of your breath is an easy gauge of if you're in **_"Rest and Digest"_** or **_"Fight or Flight"._** Learning how to focus on slowing down the breath can quickly turn on the **para-sympathetic nervous system.**

Breathing slowly into the tummy or diaphragm by making the exhalation longer than the inhalation is scientifically proven to **rebalance the body and the brain.**

A practical application that you can **begin implementing straight away** is to close your eyes and take **3 slow breaths before eating**.

Notice if **your digestion improves**, if your bloating is reduced, or your reflux disappears.

Gratitude Reset

My favorite of all **stress-reducing practices, gratitude** puts you in a high vibrational state, retraining your brain's pathways.

Scientific studies on individuals with mood disturbances found that a gratitude practice rewired their neural pathways in as little **as 2 weeks** - simply from **writing down 3 - 5 things each day that they were grateful for.**

I encourage you to **begin a gratitude practice today.** To make it easy for you, I've broken it down into 4 buckets that you can focus on when you sit down to reflect, before bed each night.

WORK	FAMILY / FRIENDS

PASSIONS	HEALTH

IT IS A SCIENTIFIC FACT THAT
GRATITUDE RECIPROCATES
- Matthew McConnaughey, Academy Award Winner

Download Reset

If you haven't already downloaded the MP3 **Positive Reset**, please do so now

SCAN ME

THE **LIGHT SHINES** IN THE DARKNESS AND THE DARKNESS
CANNOT OVERCOME IT
– John 1:5

SUPPLEMENTS

My Supplements

Are supplements necessary? It depends, on a few things.

To begin with, our modern soils are pretty depleted. Nutrients from food just aren't what they were 100 years ago. So supplementing can be a very **helpful part of any health** creating routine, **when done in tandem with nutrition changes!**

The danger, however, is when **we supplement randomly** without knowing what or why we're doing something. I often see clients come to me saying they've been taking all manner of potions, tinctures, pills but **"Nothing works."**

Over the next few pages, I'll outline the **3 main reasons** why nothing's worked – until now.

But first, use the **Supplements Audit on the following page** to reflect on what supplements you've been taking, and for how long. If you're on more than 6 supplements a day, you may need to review and streamline!

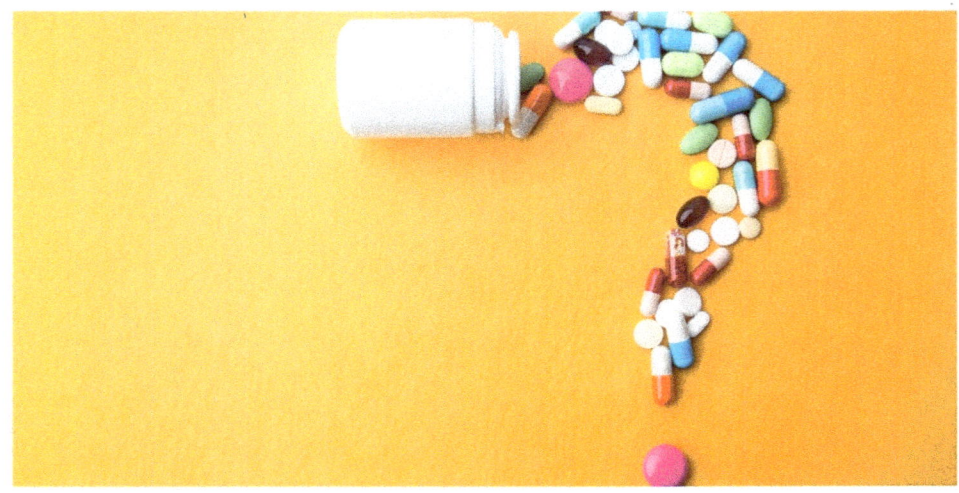

Supplements Audit

Supplement	Duration	Purpose

Supplements Audit

Supplement	Duration	Purpose

Random vs Specific

It's also likely that you haven't gotten **specific** about what supplements you need. Taking supplements **without understanding their co-factors** can be dangerous! **People who take calcium supplements** are a classic example.

Stressed people tend to leach calcium from their bones, and **calcium deposits** end up in **their joints**, their **organs,** and even their **arteries,** leading to **hypercalceimia,** kidney stones, thyroid disease, **autoimmune conditions like Raynaud's** and even cancer!

Without the **co-factors of Vitamin K2 and Magnesium,** calcium on its own does not know where to go, and **can lead to other problems.**

That's **why it's important to work with someone who understands specific supplementation, and dosing** which is usually done after lab work is conducted.

And remember, **you can't out-supplement a bad diet!**

Cheaper Isn't Better

You haven't gotten the right quality or the right form of the supplement you need, can be another reason.

Cheaper supermarket or drugstore supplements **tend to be synthetic** and encased in a substance that makes it **difficult for the gut and liver to breakdown**, which means reduced bio-availability, and **even liver damage!** They're also full of fillers, **rather than actual nutrients!**

Avoid Boots, Centrum, Costco, CVS, GNC, Holland and Barrett, Sainsburys, Seven Seas, Superdrug, Walmart, Walgreens and **any other cheaper store brands.**

Choose supplements that have been designed for maximum absorption like **FOOD-BASED** or **LIPOSOMAL. I personally have seen rapid results from using Quicksilver Scientific's products.** Their liposomal formulations are usually a liquid that you put under your tongue, that enters your bloodstream, bypassing your gut.

If you don't have access to Quicksilver, here's a top tip on how to gauge the quality of your liposomal supplements: **Clear liposomal** products are **better quality than milky** ones.

You can order from my professional dispensary on Fullscript for 15% off when you scan the QR Code below.

Time Is A Factor

You should probably also consider that **if they haven't been working so far,** maybe you haven't taken them for long enough!

Unlike medication, supplements take their time to work. When you're beginning a gut healing protocol for example, **you can expect to feel changes within the first 10 - 14 days**, but full effects can take about 3 months! After which, **you'll likely need to reduce or rotate,** because ideally you don't want to be on certain supplements unnecessarily.

Taking them for a specific time, **under supervision, after lab testing** works best!

HOW LONG HAVE I BEEN TAKING MY CURRENT SUPPLEMENTS?

WHAT BENEFITS HAVE I NOTICED?

Celebrate!

You may be at the end of this workbook, but your new story of living life abundantly is just beginning.

Remember, this journey isn't just about avoiding burnout - it's about creating a life that you are actually well enough to enjoy.

You have the power to write a new story for your health and your life.

Are you ready to claim it?

www.ingramcontent.com/pod-product-compliance
Lightning Source LLC
Chambersburg PA
CBHW051649120626
46551CB00015B/2279